The European Union

Political, Social, and Economic Cooperation

THE EUROPEAN UNION

POLITICAL, SOCIAL, AND ECONOMIC COOPERATION

The European Union
Political, Social, and Economic Cooperation

IRELAND

by
Ida Walker

Mason Crest Publishers
Philadelphia

Mason Crest Publishers Inc.
370 Reed Road, Broomall, Pennsylvania 19008
(866) MCP-BOOK (toll free)
www.masoncrest.com

First printing
1 2 3 4 5 6 7 8 9 10

Library of Congress Cataloging-in-Publication Data

Walker, Ida.
  Ireland / by Ida Walker.
       p. cm. — (The European Union)
  Includes bibliographical references and index.
    ISBN 1-4222-0051-5
    ISBN 1-4222-0038-8 (series)
1. Ireland—Juvenile literature. 2. European Union—Ireland—Juvenile literature. I. Title. II. European Union (Series) (Philadelphia, Pa.)
  DA906.W325 2006
  941.7—dc22
                              2005019674

Produced by Harding House Publishing Service, Inc.
www.hardinghousepages.com
Interior design by Benjamin Stewart.
Cover design by MK Bassett-Harvey.
Printed in the Hashemite Kingdom of Jordan.

CONTENTS

THE
EUROPEAN
UNION

GREENLAND SEA

BARENTS SEA

ICELAND
★ Reykjavik

NORWEGIAN SEA

White Sea

RUSSIA

FINLAND

Oulu

Gulf of Bothnia

Tampere

Trondheim

Turku ● Helsinki ★

Gulf of Finland

★ Tallin

ESTONIA

Bergen ●

NORWAY

Bottås

Tartu

Oslo ●

Stockholm ★

Norrköping ●

Gulf of Riga

★ Moscow

Kristiansand ●

Ventspils ●

Riga ★

LATVIA

SWEDEN

Skagerrak

Gothenburg ●

Liepaja ●

Daugavpils ●

UNITED KINGDOM

Glasgow ● ● Edinburgh

Helsingborg ●

BALTIC SEA

Klaipėda ●

LITHUANIA

Kaunas ●

DENMARK

Aalborg ●

● Belfast

Odense ●

Copenhagen ●

Malmö ●

Vilnius ★

Minsk ★

IRELAND

Irish Sea

NORTH SEA

RUSSIA

BELARUS

Killarney ●

Dublin ★

Liverpool ●

● Manchester

Gdańsk ●

● Birmingham

THE NETHERLANDS

Hamburg ●

POLAND

St. George's Channel

● London ★

The Hague ● Amsterdam ●

★ Berlin

Warsaw ★

English Channel

Rotterdam ●

Düsseldorf ●

Leipzig ●

● Wrocław

BELGIUM

Brussels ●

Cologne ●

GERMANY

Dresden ●

Kraków ●

Kyiv ★

LUXEMBOURG

Luxembourg ●

Frankfurt ●
Main

Pizen ● ● Prague

CZECH REPUBLIC

Brno ●

Košice ●

UKRAINE

● Paris

Stuttgart ●

SLOVAKIA

Nantes ●

Munich ●

Linz ●

Vienna ●

Bratislava ●

MOLDOVA

Chisinau ●

Salzburg ●

Győr ●

Budapest ●

Sea of Azov

FRANCE

Bern ●

SWITZERLAND

AUSTRIA

HUNGARY

Szeged ●

ROMANIA

Bay of Biscay

Bordeaux ●

Geneva ●

Lyons ●

Ljubljana ●

Trieste ●

Zagreb ●

Belgrade ★

★ Bucharest

BLACK SEA

Vigo ●

Bilbao ●

Milan ●

Venice ●

SLOVENIA

BOSNIA-HERCEGOVINA

Turin ●

CROATIA

Sarajevo ●

YUGOSLAVIA

● Sofia

Porto ●

Toulouse ●

Gulf de Lion

Florence ●

ADRIATIC SEA

Niš ●

BULGARIA

PORTUGAL

Marseille ●

Nice ●

ITALY

Skopje ●

MACEDONIA

Ankara ★

● Madrid

Barcelona ●

Rome ★

● Thessaloníki

Lisbon ●

Naples ●

ALBANIA

TURKEY

SPAIN

Valencia ●

TYRRHENIAN SEA

AEGEAN SEA

Faro ●

Seville ●

GREECE

Lefkoisa CYPRUS

(Nicosia)

IONIAN SEA

Athens ★

Strait of Gibraltar

Sea of Crete

Lemessos ●

SYRIA

MEDITERRANEAN SEA

Kalamata ●

LEBANON

★ Rabat

Algiers ● ★

MOROCCO

ALGERIA

Tunis ●

MALTA

● Valetta

MEDITERRANEAN SEA

JOR

ISRAEL & THE PALESTINIAN TERRITORIES

TUNISIA

Tripoli ●

Cairo ●

LIBYA

EGYPT

IRELAND

European Union Member since 1973

Carndenagh

Northern Ireland (UK)

Killala

Sligo

Castlebar

Dundalk

Longford

Drogheda

Galaway

Dublin ☆

Kingstown

Bray

Carlow

Kilkenny

Limerick

Tralee

Clonmel

Wexford

Killarney

Waterford

Cork

INTRODUCTION

Sixty years ago, Europe lay scarred from the battles of the Second World War. During the next several years, a plan began to take shape that would unite the countries of the European continent so that future wars would be inconceivable. On May 9, 1950, French Foreign Minister Robert Schuman issued a declaration calling on France, Germany, and other European countries to pool together their coal and steel production as "the first concrete foundation of a European federation." "Europe Day" is celebrated each year on May 9 to commemorate the beginning of the European Union (EU).

The EU consists of twenty-five countries, spanning the continent from Ireland in the west to the border of Russia in the east. Eight of the ten most recently admitted EU member states are former communist regimes that were behind the Iron Curtain for most of the latter half of the twentieth century.

Any European country with a democratic government, a functioning market economy, respect for fundamental rights, and a government capable of implementing EU laws and policies may apply for membership. Bulgaria and Romania are set to join the EU in 2007. Croatia and Turkey have also embarked on the road to EU membership.

While the EU began as an idea to ensure peace in Europe through interconnected economies, it has evolved into so much more today:

- Citizens can travel freely throughout most of the EU without carrying a passport and without stopping for border checks.

- EU citizens can live, work, study, and retire in another EU country if they wish.

- The euro, the single currency accepted throughout twelve of the EU countries (with more to come), is one of the EU's most tangible achievements, facilitating commerce and making possible a single financial market that benefits both individuals and businesses.

- The EU ensures cooperation in the fight against cross-border crime and terrorism.

- The EU is spearheading world efforts to preserve the environment.

- As the world's largest trading bloc, the EU uses its influence to promote fair rules for world trade, ensuring that globalization also benefits the poorest countries.

- The EU is already the world's largest donor of humanitarian aid and development assistance, providing 55 percent of global official development assistance to developing countries in 2004.

The EU is neither a nation intended to replace existing nations, nor an international organization. The EU is unique—its member countries have established common institutions to which they delegate some of their sovereignty so that decisions on matters of joint interest can be made democratically at the European level.

Europe is a continent with many different traditions and languages, but with shared values such as democracy, freedom, and social justice, cherished values well known to North Americans. Indeed, the EU motto is "United in Diversity."

Enjoy your reading. Take advantage of this chance to learn more about Europe and the EU!

Ambassador John Bruton,
Head of Delegation of the European Commission, Washington, D.C.

Ireland is intensely green

CHAPTER 1

THE LANDSCAPE

The Republic of Ireland, *Éire*, is an island on the western edge of Europe. Comprised of twenty-six independent counties, the country has an area of 27,135 square miles (70,280 sq. kilometers), slightly larger than West Virginia. The mountains and the lowlands provide the canvas for the country's forty shades of green.

GEOGRAPHY

The Caledonian and the Armorican mountains extend from Europe to meet in Ireland. The Caledonians are the older of the two ranges, and create the mountain landscape of Counties Donegal, Mayo, and Galway. The mountains are made of quartzite. Glacial valleys penetrate into the mountains. The Armorican extend into southern Ireland where they appear as sandstone ridges separated by limestone or shale valleys. The highest mountain in Ireland, the Carrantouhill (3,415 feet; 1,041 meters), is in this range.

Most of the country is a limestone-based lowland that opens into the Irish Sea. Many mountains interrupt the lowlands, which rises in the west toward the coast in County Clare, ending in the cliffs of Moher.

During the Pleistocene period, ice covered most of Ireland. When it melted away about twelve thousand years ago, glacial deposits formed **drumlins** in the greater part of the lowlands. The glacier also created conditions favorable to the growth of peat bogs.

RIVERS

The River Shannon is the longest (211 miles; 340 kilometers) of the rivers draining the lowlands. Halfway through its path, the river widens into several lakes. As it nears the sea, the River Shannon's **gradient** steepens. This is where the first attempts at **hydroelectric** power were made. Other important rivers are the Lagan, the Liffey, and the Slaney. Southern Ireland's important rivers are the Suir, the Lee, and the Blackwater.

CLIMATE

Ireland's **temperate** climate is influenced by the warm waters of the North Atlantic Drift. In Dublin, for example, the average January temperature is 45°F (7°C). In July, the average temperature is 60°F (15.5°C).

Rainfall is heaviest on westward-facing slopes. The Kerry, Mayo, and Donegal regions may receive as much as 118 inches

CONNEMARA MARBLE

In the Connemara mountains of Galway, the national gemstone of Ireland can be found—Connemara marble. According to geologists, the marble is about 500 million years old. Distinctive of the marble in this region is the serpentine stripes of varying shades of green that run throughout the marble. Stephen Walsh, whose family has quarried the marble and made handmade marble gifts for years, claims that one can see Ireland's forty shades of green in the rock.

(3,000 millimeters). In the drier regions, rainfall averages only 31 inches (785 millimeters) per year.

FLORA

Two things are immediately noticeable about Ireland's vegetation. The first is that the country is green—intensely green, a result of grasses that flourish in the mild, moist air. The second is how few trees there are. On the western coast, high winds inhibit the growth of trees. In many of the other areas, trees have been cleared to make room for farms and grazing.

In general, flora is more limited in Ireland than in other European countries. In counties Cork and

Achille Island

Ireland has a rugged coastline.

Kerry, a Mediterranean-related tree exists, the Arbutus. The mild weather and high humidity in this area encourage the growth of **lichen.** In County Clare, an Arctic-Alpine flora remains from a much colder time.

FAUNA

Ireland has twenty-seven species of mammal, in addition to the seals and whales along the coast. Native mammals include the red deer, pine marten, badger, otter, and hare. Fallow deer, rabbit, and other rodents have been introduced into the country. A small lizard is Ireland's only reptile. The country is home to three amphibians—the newt, the frog, and the toad.

Salmon, trout, char, pollan, perch, pike, and eels are found in the rivers and lakes.

A total of 380 species of wild birds are recorded in Ireland. Only about one-third of these birds actually breed there, however. Most breed elsewhere and migrate to Ireland.

QUICK FACTS: THE GEOGRAPHY OF IRELAND

Location: Western Europe, occupying five-sixths of the island of Ireland in the North Atlantic Ocean, west of Great Britain

Area: slightly larger than West Virginia
  total: 27,135 square miles (70,280 sq. km.)
  land: 26,599 square miles (68,890 sq. km.)
  water: 537 square miles (1,390 sq. km.)

Borders: UK (Northern Ireland) 224 miles (360 km.)

Climate: temperate maritime, affected by the North Atlantic Current; mild winters, cool summers; consistently humid; overcast about 50% of the time

Terrain: level to rolling interior plain surrounded by rugged hills and low mountains; sea cliffs on western coast

Elevation extremes:
  lowest point: Atlantic Ocean—0 feet (0 meters)
  highest point: Carrauntoohil—3,415 feet (1,041 meters)

Natural hazards: None

Source: www.cia.org, 2005.

Ireland's Dingle Peninsula and medieval ruins

2 CHAPTER
IRELAND'S HISTORY AND GOVERNMENT

Ireland's history can be traced back to between 7000 and 6000 BCE. The country's first inhabitants were hunter-gatherers. During the Stone Age, these people lived near the sea, where they were able to catch deer and wild boar. They also became skilled at using harpoons to hunt seals, and they ate the island's plentiful plants and shellfish.

Farming was introduced about 4000 BCE, and sheep and cattle were raised. These Stone Age farmers were the first to change Ireland's landscape as they cleared large areas of forest to make room for farming. They also built **cairns**, many of which can still be seen on the Irish landscape.

DATING SYSTEMS AND THEIR MEANING

You might be accustomed to seeing dates expressed with the abbreviations BC or AD, as in the year 1000 BC or the year AD 1900. For centuries, this dating system has been the most common in the Western world. However, since BC and AD are based on Christianity (BC stands for Before Christ and AD stands for *anno Domini*, Latin for "in the year of our Lord"), many people now prefer to use abbreviations that people from all religions can be comfortable using. The abbreviations BCE (meaning Before Common Era) and CE (meaning Common Era) mark time in the same way (for example, 1000 BC is the same year as 1000 BCE, and AD 1900 is the same year as 1900 CE), but BCE and CE do not have the same religious overtones as BC and AD.

THE CELTS

The **Celts** from eastern Europe arrived in Ireland sometime between 500 and 300 BCE and would control Ireland for 1,000 years. Their influence in language and culture survives today in such places as Galway, Cork, and Kerry.

Initially a warlike people, the Celts built stone forts across the country. The island was divided into small kingdoms, and fighting between them was commonplace. Society was class based, with kings and **aristocrats** at the top. Below them were freemen. The freemen were farmers, and their ranking on the social ladder had nothing to do with wealth; some were wealthy, while others were very poor—but all were free. Making up the lowest social class were the slaves.

Celts practiced polytheism, the worship of many gods. Their priests were called druids. Eventually, **monotheism** was introduced into Ireland, and religion would play an integral part in the country from that point on.

CHRISTIANITY COMES TO IRELAND

Sometime between third and fifth centuries, Christianity came to Ireland. How it arrived is not known with certainty, but it probably came about through trade with England and France. In 432, the future Saint Patrick arrived in Ireland. Originally from western England, Irish **marauders** kidnapped him when he was sixteen and took Patrick to Ireland to work as a slave herdsman. He escaped and returned to England

Celtic beehive-shaped houses

after six years, where he stayed until he had a religious vision. In this vision, Patrick read a letter begging him to return to Ireland. He did, and stayed there until his death in 461.

Patrick worked hard to build the Catholic Church in Ireland, not an easy endeavor. Druids often attacked him and his followers. He planned to base the Church in Ireland on the Roman model, with bishops serving as its leaders, but his plan was not followed: the Irish church instead quickly changed to a system based on monasteries with abbots as leaders. Nevertheless, Patrick

CHAPTER TWO—IRELAND'S HISTORY AND GOVERNMENT 19

and his followers built the foundation for a 300-year "golden age" of the Irish church.

Between 500 and 800 CE, the Church flourished in Ireland. Many monasteries were built all across Ireland. Ireland sent missionaries to other parts of Europe. Education and the arts thrived in the monasteries. One of the most famous art forms during this time was the making of **illuminated manuscripts**. The best-known of these books is the *Book of Kells*, completed in the ninth century.

Rock of Cashel, an ancient fortress

Today, the book is part of the collection of Trinity College in Dublin.

The Church's golden age ended with the arrival of the Vikings. In the late eighth century, the Vikings first attacked Ireland. They raided monasteries, and they abducted women and children to be slaves. But they also founded Ireland's first towns—Dublin, Cork, Waxford, and Limerick. They were skilled craftspeople and cunning traders. The Vikings were also the ones who gave Ireland its name: Eire from the **Gaelic** and the Viking word for *land*. Eventually, the Vikings intermarried with the Irish and even accepted Christianity.

THE ENGLISH COME TO IRELAND

The church regained its power and glory during the eleventh and twelfth centuries. It was reorganized into **dioceses**, and bishops, rather than abbots, became its leaders. However, Pope Adrian IV was not happy with the Irish church. He wanted to bring it under the **papacy**. In 1155, the pope gave King Henry II of England permission to invade Ireland in order to expand the influence of the Roman Church.

King Henry II had permission, but he did not immediately act on it. Instead, in 1166, King Tiernan O'Rourke forced Dermait MacMurrough,

SHAMROCKS AND SNAKES

Although not the official symbol of Ireland (the Harp is), one of the most commonly associated symbols with Ireland is the shamrock. According to legend, St. Patrick used the shamrock to teach the people of Ireland about the Holy Trinity, with each leaf representing one of its members—the Father, the Son, and the Holy Ghost.

As for the snakes—according to legend, St. Patrick rid Ireland of snakes. Ireland never had any, though. Most authorities today believe that "snakes" referred to pagans.

king of Leinster, to escape from Ireland. King MacMurrough pleaded with King Henry II for help, and Henry gave him permission to recruit soldiers from within England. Richard FitzGilbert de Clare (better known as Strongbow) agreed to help MacMurrough, on the condition that he could marry MacMurrough's daughter and succeed him as king of Leinster.

In 1170, Strongbow and his army captured Waterford and Dublin. He became king of Leinster when MacMurrough died, and King Henry II believed he was becoming too powerful. The king ordered all English soldiers to return to England by Easter 1171. In response, Strongbow agreed to submit to the king on the condition that he could retain Dublin, Waterford, and Wexford. King Henry came to Ireland in October 1171 and easily took Waterford, declaring it to be a royal city. The pope recognized him as Lord of Ireland.

In the succeeding centuries, King Henry VIII and Queen Elizabeth I would consolidate English power in Ireland.

THE DOWNFALL OF CATHOLICISM

In the early seventeenth century, King James confiscated much of Ulster, and between 1610 and 1613, large numbers of English and Scots moved onto the land taken from the native Irish. At first, newcomers to Ireland did not mix with the poor native Irish or the Old English Catholics, who rebelled in 1641. In 1642, the Anglo-Irish and the native Irish formed an alliance called the Confederation of Kilkenny. The confederation took over all Ireland except for Dublin, a few other small towns, and part of Ulster.

Ireland was pretty much left alone during the English civil war, but at its end, the victorious Oliver Cromwell and the British Parliament wanted to turn Ireland into a Protestant country. Cromwell and his forces left a trail of massacre across the country. By 1651, all of Ireland was under English control.

The English takeover meant harsh times for Catholics. In 1695, Catholics were forbidden from buying land, raising their children as Catholics, carrying firearms, and from entering the military forces or law. Though all bishops and priests were ordered to leave Ireland in 1697, many remained. In 1704, Catholic clergy remaining in Ireland were required to register and swear an oath of allegiance to the English king. In that year, a law was enacted requiring all members of the Irish Parliament and officeholders to be members of the Church of Ireland. In 1727, Catholics lost the right to vote.

By the 1760s, the Catholics had had enough, and violence erupted. Beginning in 1778, the restrictions on Catholics were repealed. In 1823, Daniel O'Connell formed the Catholic Association to force the removal of the remaining restrictions on Catholics—those dealing with serving in Parliament and holding office. Six years later, the Catholic **Emancipation** Act overturned those laws.

THE POTATO FAMINE

When Sir Walter Raleigh reportedly brought the potato to Ireland in the sixteenth century, it quickly became an important part of the Irish diet. In the 1840s, the diet of much of the population of Ireland centered around this food. The Irish depen-dence on potatoes was so complete that when a potato blight hit the country in 1845 and again in 1846 and 1847, the country was devastated. The blight lasted five years.

Approximately one million people died during the years of the famine. Each year, starvation and illnesses such as cholera, typhus, and dysentery cost hundreds of thousands their lives. Many others chose to leave Ireland, many coming to the United States. The British government did not establish relief efforts in Ireland until 1847. This delay added fuel to the Irish desire for independence.

Celtic crosses are ancient reminders of Ireland's Christian heritage.

Horse traders in Dingle

EARLY MOVES TOWARD INDEPENDENCE

By 1842, it was obvious to some in Ireland that the country would not achieve its independence through peaceful means. In that year, Young Ireland was formed to campaign for Ireland's independence, by whatever means necessary. In 1848, led by William Smith O'Brien, they fought with the Irish Constabulary in County Tipperary in the battle of the Widow McCormack's cabbage patch. O'Brien was arrested and sentenced to death, but was sent instead to Tasmania.

The Fenian movement began in 1858, but an attempted uprising in England in 1867 failed. Although the Catholic Church banned them in 1870, their activities continued.

Not all moves toward independence were violent. In 1870, Isaac Butt founded the Irish Home Government Association. The association's goal was to achieve independence for Ireland through the British Parliament. If enough politicians in favor of Irish independence could be elected Members of Parliament (MPs), Ireland could win its **sovereignty** through peaceful, political means. Although Butt was successful and many MPs were elected, he was considered to be too moderate and he lost control of the association.

In 1886, the first of the Irish Home Rule bills was introduced in Parliament, but was rejected in the House of Commons. A later one was defeated in the House of Lords. The influx of MPs supportive of Ireland did bring about some favor-

NINE FAMOUS IRISHMEN

Nine members of the Young Ireland movement were captured, tried for and convicted of treason, and sentenced to death in 1848. When the judge asked at sentencing if any of the nine wanted to say anything, Thomas Meagher replied:

> My Lord, this is our first offence, but not our last. If you will be easy with us this once, we promise on our word as gentlemen to try and do better next time. And next time—we won't be fools enough to get caught.

Irritated, the judge sentenced them to death. Worldwide protests caused Queen Victoria to commute the sentence to exile in Australia.

Almost thirty years later, it came to Queen Victoria's attention that the newly elected prime minister of Australia—Charles Duffy—was one of those men she sent to Australia. On review, it was discovered that the others had also done quite well:

Thomas Francis Meagher—Governor of Montana
Terence McManus—Brigadier General, U.S. Army
Patrick Donohue—Brigadier General, U.S. Army
Richard O'Gorman, Governor General of Newfoundland
Morris Lyne—Attorney General of Australia
Thomas D'Arcy McGee—Member of Parliament, Montreal; Minister for Agriculture and President of Council, Dominion of Canada
Michael Ireland—Attorney General of Australia (Lyne's successor)
John Mitchell—prominent New York politician

able changes. New land laws allowed thousands of tenant farmers to purchase the land they worked. The Gaelic League was formed in 1893, and Gaelic was made the official language of

Ireland again. A Home Rule bill was finally accepted in 1914, but its implementation was put on hold until the end of World War I.

While peaceful political movements toward independence were made, so were more violent tactics. Protestant opposition to Irish independence grew, and by the 1900s, Ireland appeared to be headed toward civil war. The Ulster Volunteer Force was formed in 1913, and southern nationalists formed the Irish Volunteers.

FIGHTING FOR INDEPENDENCE

Ireland knew that after the world war ended, it would have its independence. Some of the Irish Volunteers were willing to wait, but others were not. More than 100,000 broke away and called themselves the Irish National Volunteers.

The Irish Republican Brotherhood (IRB) was a secret—and powerful—organization in the early twentieth century. Many of its members sided with the Irish Volunteers. In 1915, the IRB formed a military council. An uprising was planned for Easter 1916, and the Irish Volunteers agreed to help. However, when the British Navy intercepted a German boat carrying weapons to Ireland to be used in the Easter Uprising, the volunteers changed their mind. The uprising was confined to Dublin and was destined to fail.

Politicians were not left out of the fight for independence. In the December 1918 general elections, Sinn Fein won seventy-three seats. The new MPs took a stand, however, and refused to join the British Parliament. Instead, they established their own Parliament, the Dail Eirann, in Dublin.

Despite this more peaceful political statement, violence was still evident. Just one month later, the Irish Volunteers renamed themselves the Irish Republican Army (IRA) and began a **guerrilla** war with the British. The Black and Tans, a group of former soldiers recruited by the British and sent to Ireland to assist its forces, fought a hard war with the IRA. In May 1921, the IRA burned the Customs House in Dublin. It wasn't an easy conquest, however; five members of the IRA were killed, and eighty were captured. Two months later, the war ended.

Simultaneously with the violence, the politicians had been working to solve the "Irish problem." The Government of Ireland Act was passed in the British Parliament was passed in 1920. It stated that Ireland would have two parliaments, one in the north and one in the south, but answerable to the British Parliament. In the May 1921 election of members to the parliament in south Ireland, Sinn Fein won most of the seats. But they again refused to sit in the new parliament; the Dail continued to meet.

In October 1921, the Dail appointed five members to negotiate with the British. The British prime minister demanded that the representatives sign a treaty partitioning Ireland. On threat of war, the delegates agreed. They returned home to Ireland to find the country split over the treaty. Though the Dail approved the treaty in 1922, some were willing to accept the agreement as a temporary fix, while others were **vehemently** opposed. Again war broke out, this time between the IRA and the National Army. This civil war lasted until May 1923.

A Dingle street

THE IRELAND OF THE EARLY TWENTIETH CENTURY

Life in Ireland was not easy in the 1920s and 1930s. Unemployment was high, and living conditions were overcrowded. People were still leaving the country in large numbers. Under the treaty, however, things started to get better.

Between 1925 and 1929, the government created a plan, the Shannon Scheme, to bring hydroelectricity to Irish towns. By 1943, all towns and most villages had electricity. To help reduce

THE GOOD FRIDAY AGREEMENT

The establishment of the Republic of Ireland did not mean an end to problems between the Protestants and the Catholics of Ireland. In Northern Ireland, the fighting continued to cost lives and money. Sometimes border areas of the Republic were brought into the battle. In addition, the Irish constitution called for the entire island to be part of the Republic, which did not sit well with many in Northern Ireland.

But, after many years and many false starts, the Belfast Agreement (also known as the Good Friday Agreement) was signed in April 10, 1998. This was perhaps the most significant step in trying to end the violence in Northern Ireland. Citizens of both Northern Ireland and the Republic of Ireland overwhelmingly approved the agreement in separate referendums the following month.

Among the provisions was the establishment of the North-South Ministerial Council and the North-South Implementation Body to bring about cooperation between Northern Ireland and the Republic. The British-Irish Council would be established, with representatives from the governments of the Republic of Ireland, Northern Ireland, the United Kingdom, Scotland, Wales, the Channel Islands, and the Isle of Mann. The council would meet to discuss issues of common concern.

Perhaps the most significant feature of the agreement was the revision of Articles 2 and 3 of the Constitution of Ireland. Those articles stated that the republic's "national territory consists of the whole island of Ireland, its islands and the territorial seas," and that the constitution had jurisdiction over the entire territory.

an elected president the head of state. Southern Ireland, the country known as "Irish Free State," would now be Eire or Ireland. In 1948, after years of what seemed like endless violence and conflict, Ireland (or at least the southern part of the island) was made a **republic** and was independent of Britain at last.

The Republic of Ireland was ready to take its place in the world, and it was not afraid to be a trailblazer. In 1990, Mary Robinson was the first woman to be elected president of Ireland, one of only a few women actually running a country. After a long journey to establish independence and with a government securely in place, Ireland was now determined to establish itself as a strong economic power.

the unemployment rate, the government instituted a road-building program. It also assisted in the development of industry in the 1940s.

Political movement toward independence continued as well during the 1930s and 1940s. In 1937, a new constitution was written, making

Twentieth-century Ireland

A street in Cork

3 THE ECONOMY

Ireland's long history of struggle leading to its independence was not favorable to economic development. Economic growth has come slowly. After many years of economic struggle, Ireland's trade-dependent economy has rebounded and is healthy and strong.

FROM WEAK TO STRONG

In 1949, the Industrial Development Authority (IDA) was established to promote **industrialization**. The 1950s saw a rapid growth in Ireland's economy. In the 1960s and 1970s, the economy grew at an average of 4 percent per year. The first Irish motorway and the first broadcast by Irish television both occurred in 1962. In 1973, Ireland joined the European Economic Community (EEC), the forerunner of the European Union (EU). Foreign countries began investing in Ireland, bringing with them new jobs and new businesses.

This economic boon didn't last, however, and the 1980s found the Irish economy on the skids. Unemployment had increased from 7 percent in 1979 to 17 percent in 1990. But then, in the 1990s, the economic pendulum swung upward again. The Irish economy flourished and became known as the "Celtic Tiger." By 2000, unemployment was an enviable less than 4 percent.

The Irish economy was not immune to the worldwide economic slowdown of 2001, especially in high-tech exports, but it continued to grow, although at a slower rate. Today, the Irish economy is growing at a rate of 7 percent per year.

Irish per capita **gross domestic product (GDP)** is 10 percent above the four

---

QUICK FACTS: THE ECONOMY OF IRELAND

Gross Domestic Product (GDP): US$126.4 billion

GDP per capita: US$31,900

Industries: steel, lead, zinc, silver, aluminum, barite, and gypsum mining processing; food products, brewing, textiles, clothing; chemicals, pharmaceuticals; machinery, rail transportation equipment, passenger and commercial vehicles, ship construction and refurbishment; glass and crystal; software, tourism

Agriculture: turnips, barley, potatoes, sugar beets, wheat; beef, dairy products

Export commodities: machinery and equipment, computers, chemicals, pharmaceuticals; live animals, animal products

Export partners: U.S. 20.2%, UK 17.5%, Belgium 14.8%, Germany 7.5%, France 5.9%, Italy 4.5%, Netherlands 4.4%

Import commodities: data processing equipment, other machinery and equipment, chemicals; petroleum and petroleum products, textiles, clothing

Import partners: UK 35.2%, U.S. 13.5%, Germany 8.9%, Netherlands 4.3%

Currency: euro (EUR)

Currency exchange rate: US$1 = .84 EUR (July 4, 2005)

Note: All figures are from 2004 unless otherwise noted.
Source: www.cia.org, 2005.

Farming is important to Ireland's economy.

largest European economies and is second-highest in the EU (behind Luxembourg). Since the 1990s, the government has established programs to reduce price and wage inflation, reduce government spending, increase the skills of the country's labor force, and promote foreign investment.

AGRICULTURE

Agriculture has long played significant roles in Ireland's economy. Small and medium-sized farms and fields still dominate the Irish landscape. Turnips, barley, potatoes, sugar beets, and wheat are the primary crops grown today. Beef and dairy products are also important to the Irish economy.

As the Irish economy has developed, agriculture's importance has lessened in the overall picture. Agriculture and agricultural-related industries

Haystacks in the Wicklow Mountains

employ only 8 percent of the population. Five percent of the GDP is provided by agriculture and related businesses.

INDUSTRIAL AND SERVICE SECTORS

Industrial and the **service sectors** have surpassed agriculture in importance to the Irish economy. Today, industry makes up 46 percent of the GDP and accounts for about 80 percent of the country's exports. An estimated 29 percent of Ireland's workforce is employed in industry. The service sector provides 49 percent of the GDP and employs about 63 percent of Ireland's population.

To develop Ireland's industry, the government at first enacted **protectionist** policies. Their goal was to establish Irish-owned industries to serve the domestic market. Policies changed in the 1950s, when the benefits of free trade and foreign investment were realized. The United States, Britain, and Germany have been the largest investors. Industry has been concentrated in Dublin, but the Irish government is to encourage industrial development in other areas.

Ireland's primary industries are metals and engineering, food products, rail transportation equipment, ship construction and refurbishment, software, and tourism.

The growth in the service sector has played an important role in the growth of Ireland's economy in recent years. Principal service categories include educational and medical services, retail and wholesale distribution, public administration and defense, and the insurance, finance, and business service group. Because of the need to be near consumers, most of the growth in the service sector has occurred in urban areas such as Dublin.

TOURISM

In the years following World War II, tourism experienced significant growth. More than three million people visit Ireland yearly. Most of the tourists come from Great Britain, but increasing numbers come from the United States. A substantial number of Irish tourists travel within their own country.

The relaxed atmosphere, friendly people, clean countryside, and attractive scenery are major tourist attractions. The country's literary and historical features also draw tourists. Many people visit Ireland to discover their ancestry.

The coastal areas see the most tourism, but increasing numbers of tourists are discovering the beauty of Ireland's interior.

TRANSPORTATION

The primary method of travel in Ireland is by private vehicle on roadways; there are 59,488 miles (95,736 kilometers) of highways, all paved, in Ireland. Public buses are available in some areas, but their paths through the countryside are often meandering.

Unlike many European countries, Ireland's road network was designed for a population larger than it currently has. As a result, traffic is light

by European standards. The amount is increasing, however, and there is congestion in the major urban areas and tourist attractions.

The railway system was developed in the nineteenth century. Because of competition from road transportation, some branch lines closed, along with some main routes and smaller rail stations. Today, there are 2,058 miles (3.312 kilometers) of rail tracks. Dublin is the main destination for rail traffic.

Seaports are important to Ireland's economy, since most goods and many passengers go by sea. The main seaports are on the east and south coasts. Most traffic goes through Larne, Belfast, and Dublin.

The primary international airports are at Dublin and Shannon. Flights are available to most major British cities and to mainland European countries. Transatlantic flights are routed through Shannon. The growth of Ireland's national airline, Aer Lingus, reflects the increase in air transport to and from Ireland. Aer Lingus carries more than four million passengers yearly.

Although Ireland's economy is progressive and prosperous, complete with Internet access, much of the country's culture continues to reflect its history and values.

Cork is a hub for Irish culture and population.

4 IRELAND'S PEOPLE AND CULTURE

CHAPTER

Ireland is a country of more than four million people. Although the land has historically become home to immigrants moving westward across the European continent, the Irish are primarily of Celtic origin.

Men in Cork

Roman Catholicism is the official religion of the Republic of Ireland; more than 91 percent are Roman Catholic, but regular attendance at mass has declined, as has strict adherence to the church's rules. Most of the seminaries have closed. The influence of the Roman Catholic Church on government has waned as well, as shown in the legalization of divorce; the first legal Irish divorce was obtained in 1997.

Membership in the Church of Ireland, the second-largest religion, is also declining—most of its rural churches and some of those in urban areas

have closed—and declining membership is a characteristic of Ireland's already small Jewish population. The only religions that have seen an expansion are Islam and born-again Christian groups. These increases reflect the characteristics of Ireland's immigrant population.

EDUCATION

Education is important to the Irish; 90 percent of all children attend secondary education, and 50 percent attend third-level educational institutes. Though many schools are still church affiliated, the number of **multidenominational** and coeducational schools has increased in recent years. Parents can elect for their children to be taught in English, Gaelic, or other modern European languages. Parents also have a constitutional right to homeschool their children. All public schools are state funded. Educational opportunities have expanded as

well for adults who want to return to school. Ninety-nine percent of Ireland's population age fifteen and older can read and write.

The Irish educational system is divided into three levels. The first is primary school. Although children are not required to attend school until they

---

QUICK FACTS: THE PEOPLE OF IRELAND

Population: 4,015,676
Ethnic groups: Celtic, English
Age structure:
　　0–14 years: 20.9%
　　15–64 years: 67.5%
　　65 years and over: 11.5%
Population growth rate: 1.16%
Birth rate: 14.47 births/1,000 pop.
Death rate: 7.85 deaths/1,000 pop.
Migration rate: 4.93 migrant(s)/1,000 pop.
Infant mortality rate: 5.39 deaths/1,000 live births
Life expectancy at birth:
　　Total population: 77.56 years
　　Males: 74.95 years
　　Females: 80.34 years
Total fertility rate: 1.87 children born/woman
Religions: Roman Catholic 91.6%, Church of Ireland 2.5%, other 5.9% (1998)
Languages: English (official), Gaelic spoken mainly in areas along the western seaboard
Literacy rate: 99% (2003 est.)

Note: All figures are from 2005 unless otherwise noted.
Source: www.cia.org, 2005.

are age six, many start primary school at age four.

After completing grade 6, students advance to secondary school. Students are generally Leaving Certificate on completion of the second level. Students have a choice of attending universities, institutes of technology, colleges of education, and private colleges.

"DANNY BOY"

Almost everyone has heard the song "Danny Boy." It's played and sung, often badly, many times around St. Patrick's Day. Bagpipes often accompany the tune at funerals, especially of firefighters. Ironically, however, many Irish immigrants never hear the song until they come to the United States.

"Danny Boy" is one of more than one hundred songs with the same tune, "Londonderry Aire." Frederic Edward Weatherly, an English lawyer, wrote the words, and as far as can be determined, he was never in Ireland. His first attempt included words and music, but it was unsuccessful. In 1912, his sister-in-law sent him the tune "Londonderry Aire," and he noticed how well the melody and words went together: "Danny Boy" was born.

about age twelve and graduate at age seventeen or eighteen, after they complete two state exams. The secondary school year begins in September and runs through June. The secondary level includes secondary schools, **vocational** schools, and community or comprehensive schools. Most students attend secondary schools. Vocational and community or comprehensive schools offer academic and technical classes. Adults returning to school often attend community or comprehensive schools.

If a student wants to attend a university—the third level—she will have to accumulate a certain number of points in addition to receiving a

MUSIC

Music is a mainstay of Irish culture. Sing-a-longs in Irish pubs appear in many movies, and this is one tradition that exists in real life. Internationally known Irish singers include the Pogues, Elvis Costello, Sinéad O'Connor, and Enya. Irish tenors are legendary in opera. Some of the more recent ones include Ronan Tynan and Anthony Kearns. Bob Geldof, formerly of the Boomtown Rats, organized 1985's Live Aid concert, as well as 2005's Live 8 concert. Perhaps the best-known Irish music group is U2, led by Bono (Paul Hewson). Like Geldof, Bono has moved beyond music to become an activist.

LITERATURE

Although music is a strong element of Irish culture, perhaps Irish authors have made the greatest impact on the rest of the world. Oscar Wilde, George Bernard Shaw, Samuel Beckett, and Jonathan Swift are some of the writers who have influenced literature worldwide.

A bar near Cork

Some critics consider James Joyce to be the most influential author of the twentieth century. Many readers of his *Ulysses* come to Dublin to retrace the events of Bloomsday.

Contemporary Irish authors include J. P. Donleavy, Brendan Behan, and Roddy Doyle. Frank McCourt, author of *Angela's Ashes*, his mother's story of life in Ireland, was born in the United States but moved to Ireland when he was four.

potatoes top a lamb shepherd's pie. Other root vegetables such as carrots, leeks, and turnips are also important parts of the Irish diet.

A TRADITIONAL CORNED BEEF AND CABBAGE DINNER FOR ST. PATRICK'S DAY

Well, if that's what you eat to celebrate St. Patrick's Day, you should probably not celebrate it in Ireland. Salted beef would have been a luxury in times past. You're more likely to find seafood than corned beef served in Irish homes on St. Patrick's Day.

FOOD AND DRINK

Despite common misperceptions, the Irish diet centers on meat—beef, pork, and lamb. Food is hearty, laborer's fare. Stews and other dishes that can be cooked all day are common in rural areas. Stews are often served with chunks of Irish soda bread.

In early times, beef was a luxury seldom served except among the upper class. Lamb and pork were more likely found on the tables of average Irish families. Today, beef is less expensive and has become a major part of the Irish diet.

From the time of the Celts first occupation of Ireland, oats made up a large proportion of the Irish diet. They continued to be an important food staple after potatoes came to Ireland. In time, however, potatoes replaced oats in the diet of many Irish. Recently, however, oats have made a comeback in the diets of health-conscious Irish.

The Irish diet has not eliminated potatoes. They are often served as part of a stew. Mashed

Many Irish enjoy their **stout**, a type of beer. Whiskey is another popular spirit. There is also a small but growing wine industry. Tea is another popular beverage, generally served hot or at room temperature.

SYMBOLS AND LEGENDS

Symbols and legends have been a part of Irish culture since the country began. Many, such as the leprechaun, are well known. Some others are not.

Some symbols evolved through necessity. The Aran stitch pattern, perhaps the best known of the patterns for Irish knitted sweaters, developed generations ago on the Aran Islands at the mouth of Galway Bay. Life was hard for those who fished the cold and rough waters of the Atlantic. Each **clan** designed a unique knitting pattern based on the elements used in the work of the fishermen—cables representing ropes, basketweave representing the **creel**. The sweaters provided much-

Ireland's magical land

needed warmth for the fishermen. The pattern also provided a means of identification should a fisherman be killed and traditional forms of identification prove difficult.

The Claddagh is another important symbol of Ireland. According to legend, when Richard Joyes (as he spelled Joyce) sailed for the West Indies, he was captured by an Algerian pirate and sold into slavery. His new master, a goldsmith, taught his craft to Joyes. Joyes's skill earned him the respect of his master. After King William III **ascended** to the English throne, he sent an ambassador to Algiers to demand the immediate release of all British subjects. When his master learned that Joyes was to be released, he offered the Irishman the hand of his only daughter in hope that he might stay. Richard declined, and shortly afterward he returned to the small village of Claddagh, where he became a successful jeweler. In most versions of the legend, his most famous creation—the Claddagh ring—was designed for the woman he left behind when he was captured. The heart symbolizes love; the crown, loyalty; and the hands, friendship. Some of Joyes's rings, bearing his jeweler's mark, still exist.

LEPRECHAUNS

Almost everyone has heard of leprechauns. The name leprechaun may come from *leath bhrogan*, Irish for shoemaker or *luacharma'n*, Irish for pygmy. The very old, very small leprechauns usually appear very intoxicated, generally from some kind of home brew.

According to legends, these wee folk are the self-appointed guardians of a treasure left by the Danes as they invaded Ireland. The leprechauns generally avoid humans, who they consider foolish, flighty, and greedy. If a human happens to capture one of the leprechauns, he will promise great fortune if the human releases him.

Each leprechaun carries two leather pouches. In one there is a magical silver shilling. Every time the leprechaun spends it, the coin returns to the purse. The other bag holds a gold coin the leprechaun uses to bribe himself out of difficult situations. Once the coin is given, however, it turns to leaves or ashes.

Leprechauns are seldom—if ever—seen outside Ireland. However, thanks to the Internet, you can keep an eye out for one: www.irelandseye.com/leprechaun/leprechaun.html. Just remember to report any sightings to the Webmaster.

View of Cork

5 THE CITIES

Ireland has a history of small towns and villages. Even today, villages rather than large cities characterize the country. Even the country's largest city has a population of just over one million.

DUBLIN

The capital and country's largest city, Dublin (in Irish, *Baile Átha Cliath*) is located in the east-central part of the country, on the Irish Sea. The population of the Dublin metropolitan area is 1,020,000, though the city itself is much smaller.

Dublin is the center of Ireland's transportation network. Dublin Port is the country's most important seaport. Most of the country's airline passengers go through Dublin Airport.

Agricultural products, whiskey, and stout are the area's chief exports. The city's chief industries include brewing, textile manufacturing, and glass. The Dáil Éireann, the Irish legislature, is headquartered here.

Dublin is the intellectual capital of Ireland. Among the major attractions is the University of Dublin, also known as Trinity College. Steeped in historical traditions, its library holds the *Book of Kells*, as well as a copy of every book published in the British Isles. Dublin City University is the newest of Ireland's universities. It specializes in engineering, business, and science. The Royal College of Surgeons in Ireland is an independent medical school located in the city's center. The Dublin Institute of Technology is the technical college and the country's largest nonuniversity third-level institution.

Dublin Castle, built around 1220 but renovated many times since, was once home to the lord lieutenants of Ireland. It now houses government offices and the Charles Beatty Library.

Culture is easy to find in Dublin. James Joyce's *Ulysses* was set here. His extensive details draw many tourists to Dublin to re-create the tale. For art lovers, the National Print Museum of Ireland, the Irish Museum of Modern Art, the National Gallery of Ireland, the Hugh Lane Municipal Gallery, and three branches of the National Museum of Ireland are located in Ireland.

Another type of culture is also strong in Dublin—the night life. Temple Bar is a renowned destination for many tourists. Pub crawls are popular with locals as well as tourists. A truly **metropolitan** city, there is a growing homosexual community.

CORK

Corcaigh in Irish, Cork is the second-largest city in the Republic of Ireland, with a 2002 population of 186,239. An island in the middle of the River Lee, which flows through the city, forms the main part of the city's center.

The city is a historic one; its charter was granted more than eight hundred years ago. It began even earlier as a monastery. At one ti was completely walled. The city has b many times in its history.

The city of Cork exhibits impressiv of architecture. Patrick Street, the

Doors in Dublin

street, was remodeled in recent years. Much of the broad avenue has been blocked to vehicular traffic and dedicated to pedestrians. Many financial institutions and offices are located on Grand Parade, a tree-lined part of the avenue.

South Mall is home to Cork's old financial center. Many of the banks located there date back to the nineteenth century Georgian style. Also on the mall is one of Ireland's tallest buildings, the modern County Hall tower. The Mental Hospital, built

The canal that runs through Cork

during the reign of Queen Victoria, sits across the river, and is Ireland's longest building.

The church tower of Shandon is Cork's most famous building. Its north and east sides are faced in red sandstone, and the west and south in white sandstone. The church's clock tower is known as "The Four Liars"; from the base of the building, each clock face seems to show a different time. The general public is allowed to ring the church bells.

Also of note is the English Market. The market dates back to 1610, but the present covered building was built in 1786. Vendors sell fresh fish, fruit, meat, spices, and specialty foods.

Culture is alive and well in Cork. As a matter of fact, it was named the European Capital of Culture for 2005. City life is punctuated by music, theater, dance, and film. Concerts, a film festival, and jazz festival add to the cultural life, as does the Crawford Art Gallery and the Lewis Glucksman Gallery.

Education also has a strong base in Cork. University College Cork is one of Ireland's seven universities. Courses offered include art, law, engineering, medicine, and science. The *Sunday Times* named University College Cork the Irish University of the Year 2003–2004.

Nautical studies are offered at the Cork Institute of Technology. The institute also offers many third-level courses.

GALWAY

Gaillimh—Galway—is the largest city in the county of Connacht. Located on the west coast of Ireland, and on the northeast corner of Galway Bay, the Corrib River ␣e city in two. The Connemara mountain ␣to the west, and a rolling plain is to the ␣ording to a 2002 census, Galway has ␣ion of about 66,000.

␣en "tribes" brought the walled city of ␣o its prominence, hence its nickname the City of Tribes. An **Anglo-Norman** city, it had difficulties with its Gaelic neighbors. The city was on the wrong side in several battles, and it declined in importance until Ireland's economic growth of the late twentieth century.

Galway's primary industries are agriculture and fishing. Some marble is quarried, and light manufacturing has begun. Galway crystal is earning a worldwide reputation for its beauty and quality.

Cultural events are held in Galway throughout the year. These include arts festivals, film festivals, music festivals, and an oyster festival. It is also the host of the famous Galway Races in August.

There are two higher education facilities in Galway, the Galway-Mayo Institute of Technology and the National University of Ireland. The city is also the location of the Central Applications Office, the central clearinghouse for undergraduate college and university applications for the entire republic.

The EU flag

6 THE FORMATION OF THE EUROPEAN UNION

The EU is an economic and political confederation of twenty-five European nations. Member countries abide by common foreign and security policies and cooperate on judicial and domestic affairs. The confederation, however, does not replace existing states or governments. Each of the twenty-five member states is *autonomous*, but they have all agreed to establish some common institutions and to hand over some of their own decision-making powers to these international bodies. As a result, decisions on matters that interest all member states can be made democratically, accommodating everyone's concerns and interests.

Today, the EU is the most powerful regional organization in the world. It has evolved from a primarily economic organization to an increasingly political one. Besides promoting economic cooperation, the EU requires that its members uphold fundamental values of peace and **solidarity**, human dignity, freedom, and equality. Based on the principles of democracy and the rule of law, the EU respects the culture and organizations of member states.

HISTORY

The seeds of the EU were planted more than fifty years ago in a Europe reduced to smoking piles of rubble by two world wars. European nations suffered great financial difficulties in the postwar period. They were struggling to get back on their feet and realized that another war would cause further hardship. Knowing that internal conflict was hurting all of Europe, a drive began toward European cooperation.

France took the first historic step. On May 9, 1950 (now celebrated as Europe Day), Robert Schuman, the French foreign minister, proposed the coal and steel industries of France and West Germany be coordinated under a single supranational authority. The proposal, known as the Treaty

of Paris, attracted four other countries—Belgium, Luxembourg, the Netherlands, and Italy—and resulted in the 1951 formation of the European Coal and Steel Community (ECSC). These six countries became the founding members of the EU.

In 1957, European cooperation took its next big leap. Under the Treaty of Rome, the European Economic Community (EEC) and the European Atomic Energy Community (EURATOM) were formed. Informally known as the Common Market, the EEC promoted joining the national economies into a single European economy. The 1965 Treaty of Brussels (more commonly referred to as the Merger Treaty) united these various treaty organizations under a single umbrella, the European Community (EC).

In 1992, the Maastricht Treaty (also known as the Treaty of the European Union) was signed in Maastricht, the Netherlands, signaling the birth of the EU as it stands today. **Ratified** the following year, the Maastricht Treaty provided f⸱ banking system, a common currency ⸱ replace the national currencies, a leg⸱ of the EU, and a framework for exp⸱

The EU's united economy has allowed it to become a worldwide financial power.

EU's political role, particularly in the area of foreign and security policy.

By 1993, the member countries completed their move toward a single market and agreed to participate in a larger common market, the European Economic Area, established in 1994.

The EU, headquartered in Brussels, Belgium, reached its current member strength in spurts. In

1973, Denmark, Ireland, and the United Kingdom joined the six founding members of the EC. They were followed by Greece in 1981, and Portugal and Spain in 1986. The 1990s saw the unification of the two Germanys, and as a result, East Germany entered the EU fold. Austria, Finland, and Sweden joined the EU in 1995, bringing the total number of member states to fifteen. In 2004, the EU nearly doubled its size when ten countries—Cyprus, the Czech Republic, Estonia, Hungary, Latvia, Lithuania, Malta, Poland, Slovakia, and Slovenia—became members.

THE EU FRAMEWORK

The EU's structure has often been compared to a "roof of a temple with three columns." As established by the Maastricht Treaty, this three-pillar framework encompasses all the policy areas—or pillars—of European cooperation. The three pillars of the EU are the European Community, the Common Foreign and Security Policy (CFSP), and Police and Judicial Co-operation in Criminal Matters.

QUICK FACTS: THE EUROPEAN UNION

Number of Member Countries: 25

Official Languages: 20—Czech, Danish, Dutch, English, Estonian, Finnish, French, German, Greek, Hungarian, Italian, Latvian, Lithuanian, Maltese, Polish, Portuguese, Slovak, Slovenian, Spanish, and Swedish; additional language for treaty purposes: Irish Gaelic

Motto: *In Varietate Concordia* (United in Diversity)

European Council's President: Each member state takes a turn to lead the council's activities for 6 months.

European Commission's President: José Manuel Barroso (Portugal)

European Parliament's President: Josep Borrell (Spain)

Total Area: 1,502,966 square miles (3,892,685 sq. km.)

Population: 454,900,000

Population Density: 302.7 people/square mile (116.8 people/sq. km.)

GDP: €9.61.1012

Per Capita GDP: €21,125

Formation:
- Declared: February 7, 1992, with signing of the Maastricht Treaty
- Recognized: November 1, 1993, with the ratification of the Maastricht Treaty

Community Currency: Euro. Currently 12 of the 25 member states have adopted the euro as their currency.

Anthem: "Ode to Joy"

Flag: Blue background with 12 gold stars arranged in a circle

Official Day: Europe Day, May 9

Source: europa.eu.int

PILLAR ONE

The European Community pillar deals with economic, social, and environmental policies. It is a body consisting of the European Parliament, European Commission, European Court of Justice, Council of the European Union, and the European Courts of Auditors.

PILLAR TWO

The idea that the EU should speak with one voice in world affairs is as old as the European integration process itself. Toward this end, the Common Foreign and Security Policy (CFSP) was formed in 1993.

PILLAR THREE

The cooperation of EU member states in judicial and criminal matters ensures that its citizens enjoy the freedom to travel, work, and live securely and safely anywhere within the EU. The third pillar—Police and Judicial Co-operation in Criminal Matters—helps to protect EU citizens from international crime and to ensure equal access to justice and fundamental rights across the EU.

The flags of the EU's nations:

top row, left to right
Belgium, the Czech Republic, Denmark, Germany, Estonia, Greece

second row, left to right
Spain, France, Ireland, Italy, Cyprus, Latvia

third row, left to right
Lithuania, Luxembourg, Hungary, Malta, the Netherlands, Austria

bottom row, left to right
Poland, Portugal, Slovenia, Slovakia, Finland, Sweden, United Kingdom

ECONOMIC STATUS

As of May 2004, the EU had the largest economy in the world, followed closely by the United States. But even though the EU continues to enjoy a trade surplus, it faces the twin problems of high unemployment rates and **stagnancy**.

The 2004 addition of ten new member states is expected to boost economic growth. EU membership is likely to stimulate the economies of these relatively poor countries. In turn, their prosperity growth will be beneficial to the EU.

THE EURO

The EU's official currency is the euro, which came into circulation on January 1, 2002. The shift to the euro has been the largest monetary changeover in the world. Twelve countries—Belgium, Germany, Greece, Spain, France, Ireland, Italy, Luxembourg, the Netherlands, Finland, Portugal, and Austria—have adopted it as their currency.

SINGLE MARKET

Within the EU, laws of member states are harmonized and domestic policies are coordinated to create a larger, more-efficient single market.

The chief features of the EU's internal policy on the single market are:

- free trade of goods and services

- a common EU competition law that controls anticompetitive activities of companies and member states

- removal of internal border control and harmonization of external controls between member states

- freedom for citizens to live and work anywhere in the EU as long as they are not dependent on the state

- free movement of **capital** between member states

- harmonization of government regulations, corporation law, and trademark registration

- a single currency

- coordination of environmental policy

- a common agricultural policy and a common fisheries policy

- a common system of indirect taxation, the value-added tax (VAT), and common customs duties and **excise**

- funding for research

- funding for aid to disadvantaged regions

The EU's external policy on the single market specifies:

- a common external **tariff** and a common position in international trade negotiations

- funding of programs in other Eastern European countries and developing countries

COOPERATION AREAS

EU member states cooperate in other areas as well. Member states can vote in European Parliament elections. Intelligence sharing and cooperation in criminal matters are carried out through EUROPOL and the Schengen Information System.

The EU is working to develop common foreign and security policies. Many member states are resisting such a move, however, saying these are sensitive areas best left to individual member states. Arguing in favor of a common approach to security and foreign policy are countries like France and Germany, who insist that a safer and more secure Europe can only become a reality under the EU umbrella.

One of the EU's great achievements has been to create a boundary-free area within which people, goods, services, and money can move around freely; this ease of movement is sometimes called "the four freedoms." As the EU grows in size, so do the challenges facing it—and yet its fifty-year history has amply demonstrated the power of cooperation.

Europe is proud of its "bright idea," a union with economic and political power.

The EU believes that it can use its power to act as a "lighthouse" for the rest of the world.

Key EU Institutions

Five key institutions play a specific role in the EU.

The European Parliament

The European Parliament (EP) is the democratic voice of the people of Europe. Directly elected every five years, the Members of the European Parliament (MEPs) sit not in national **blocs** but in political groups representing the seven main political parties of the member states. Each group reflects the political ideology of the national parties to which its members belong. Some MEPs are not attached to any political group.

Council of the European Union

The Council of the European Union (formerly known as the Council of Ministers) is the main legislative and decision-making body in the EU. It brings together the nationally elected representatives of the member-state governments. One minister from each of the EU's member states attends council meetings. It is the forum in which government representatives can assert their interests and reach compromises. Increasingly, the Council of the European Union and the EP are acting together as colegislators in decision-making processes.

EUROPEAN COMMISSION

The European Commission does much of the day-to-day work of the EU. Politically independent, the commission represents the interests of the EU as a whole, rather than those of individual member states. It drafts proposals for new European laws, which it presents to the EP and the Council of the European Union. The European ssion makes sure EU decisions are implemented properly and supervises the way EU re spent. It also sees that everyone abides European treaties and European law.

EU member-state governments choose the an Commission president, who is then ed by the EP. Member states, in consultah the incoming president, nominate the ropean Commission members, who must approved by the EP. The commission is

appointed for a five-year term, but can be dismissed by the EP. Many members of its staff work in Brussels, Belgium.

COURT OF JUSTICE

Headquartered in Luxembourg, the Court of Justice of the European Communities consists of one independent judge from each EU country. This court ensures that the common rules decided in the EU are understood and followed uniformly by all the members. The Court of Justice settles disputes over how EU treaties and legislation are interpreted. If national courts are in doubt about how to apply EU rules, they must ask the Court of Justice. Individuals can also bring proceedings against EU institutions before the court.

COURT OF AUDITORS

EU funds must be used legally, economically, and for their intended purpose. The Court of Auditors, an independent EU institution located in Luxembourg, is responsible for overseeing how EU money is spent. In effect, these auditors help European taxpayers get better value for the money that has been channeled into the EU.

OTHER IMPORTANT BODIES

1. European Economic and Social Committee: expresses the opinions of organized civil society on economic and social issues

2. Committee of the Regions: expresses the opinions of regional and local authorities

3. European Central Bank: responsible for monetary policy and managing the euro

4. European Ombudsman: deals with citizens' complaints about mismanagement by any EU institution or body

5. European Investment Bank: helps achieve EU objectives by financing investment projects

Together with a number of agencies and other bodies completing the system, the EU's institutions have made it the most powerful organization in the world.

EU MEMBER STATES

In order to become a member of the EU, a country must have a stable democracy that guarantees the rule of law, human rights, and protection of minorities. It must also have a functioning market economy as well as a civil service capable of applying and managing EU laws.

The EU provides substantial financial assistance and advice to help candidate countries prepare themselves for membership. As of October 2004, the EU has twenty-five member states. Bulgaria and Romania are likely to join in 2007, which would bring the EU's total population to nearly 500 million.

In December 2004, the EU decided to open negotiations with Turkey on its proposed membership. Turkey's possible entry into the EU has been fraught with controversy. Much of this controversy has centered on Turkey's human rights record and the divided island of Cyprus. If allowed to join the EU, Turkey would be its most-populous member state.

The 2004 expansion was the EU's most ambitious enlargement to date. Never before has the EU embraced so many new countries, grown so much in terms of area and population, or encompassed so many different histories and cultures. As the EU moves forward into the twenty-first century, it will undoubtedly continue to grow in both political and economic strength.

Slea Head on the Dingle Peninsula

7 IRELAND IN THE EUROPEAN UNION

Ireland was part of the first expansion of the EU in 1973. In the years since, Ireland has played an

THE IRISH ECONOMY AND THE EU

During the 1990s, the EU provided much-needed economic assistance to Ireland. This boost gave Ireland the ability to stabilize their economy and to seek foreign investment, making the country's economy truly international. Despite an often-

THE EU AND NORTHERN IRELAND

The EU has a special presence in Northern Ireland through its Programme for Peace and Reconciliation. This EU-funded program takes in Northern Ireland and the Republic of Ireland's border regions of Cavan, Donegal, Leitrim, Louth, Monaghan, and Sligo.

Reconciliation between Northern Ireland and the Republic was a component of the Good Friday Agreement. The principal aim of the Programme for Peace and Reconciliation is to facilitate that reconciliation and to help build a peaceful, stable society. Funding through the program is available for businesses, women, young people, the farming community, and other community groups. Between 2000 and 2004, more than €704 million were available for projects. Among the successful projects was the cross-border Drake Music Project, which targeted people with disabilities.

booming economy, Ireland's economic practices have not been without criticism from the EU. Ireland's close economic relationship with the United States has caused concern among some ing the EU. In 2001, the EU reprimanded Ireland for a budget that could have fueled inflation.

IRELAND AND EXPANSION

In 2002, Ireland became the last EU member state to approve expansion plans, which extended membership offers to Eastern European countries. This was the second time Ireland had voted on the issue. In the first vote, in 2001, Ireland rejected expansion plans. Though it could have ended there, Irish prime minister Bertie Ahern scheduled a second vote, which passed by an almost 2 to 1 margin. If Ireland had again rejected the referendum, the EU's growth plans would have ended for the time.

IRELAND AND THE EU PRESIDENCY

In January 2004, Ireland took its six-month turn at the presidency of the EU. One of the most significant events during its term was the accession of ten new member states in May, the largest expansion of the EU.

Shortly before the end of Ireland's turn as president, the European Council agreed on the Constitutional Treaty for Europe. The treaty was signed by the EU member states in October.

In 2005, the constitution went before the citizens of the member states. As of this writing, the ratification of the treaty appears to be in doubt. Rather

Farm in the Wicklow Mountains

Castle north of Shannon

than run the risk of defeating the constitution, Ireland has postponed voting on ratification. Major concerns of Irish citizens include the possibility that a Federal Europe would be created. There is also concern that Ireland's treasured neutrality would be threatened.

When Ireland assumed the presidency of the EU, one goal was to make it easier for citizens of member states to get information about what was happening in the EU. A Web site was created, and people worldwide now have access to almost-immediate information.

A Calendar of Irish Festivals

Ireland never overlooks an opportunity to celebrate. With an overwhelmingly Roman Catholic population, Ireland celebrates many religious holidays. But, nonreligious holidays are celebrated as well. Many towns and villages have their own festivals. Music, food, and drink are often available in abundance at these festivals.

January: January 1, **New Year's Day** is a public holiday. It is a time of celebration as well as one of reflection on how to be a better person in the new year. **Epiphany**, a Christian festival celebrating the arrival of the Three Wise Men to Jesus's manger, is celebrated on January 6.

February: February 1 is **St. Brigid's Day**, in honor of the pagan goddess of fire and fertility who became a saint. In many homes a loaf of bread is put on the windowsill for Saint Brigid and an ear of corn left their for her white cow. **Candlemas** is celebrated on February 2. Candles are taken to church to be blessed. The **Dublin International Film Festival** is also held in February.

March/April: St. Patrick's Day, perhaps the best known of Irish holidays, is held on March 17. Food, music, and good times are characteristics of celebrations held in honor of Ireland's patron saint. In Ireland, it is a public holiday—a day off of work and school. **Easter** can fall in either March or April. It begins on **Good Friday** and ends on **Easter Monday**. It is celebrated much like it is in North America, but is a public holiday, with no work or school.

May: The first Monday in May is **May Day**, a public holiday.

June: June 1 is a public holiday, formerly celebrated as **Whitmonday**, the day following the Christian Pentecost. June 16 celebrates perhaps the best-known work of one of Ireland's favorite sons, James Joyce. **Bloomsday**, held in Dublin, features reenactments of Joyce's *Ulysses*, the site of the book. Also held in June is the yearly **Writers' Week**, held in County Kerry.

August: Ireland is known for equestrian activities, and August is the world-renowned **Dublin Horse Show** and horse races in Tralee. Also in Tralee during August is the **Rose of Tralee International Festival**. People come from the world over to sample Irish music and food, and watch parades and extravagant fireworks displays. The festival is capped with the crowning of the new Rose of Tralee. At Killorglin, in County Kerry, the **Puck Fair** signals a time of massive amounts of drinking and eating.

September: The arts are featured in September, with the **Film Festival** in Cork.

October: Dublin hosts its annual **Theatre Festival** in October. At Kinsale in County Cork, food again takes the stage, but this time it's with **Ireland's Gourmet Festival**. October 31 is **Halloween**, and it is celebrated much the same way as in North America. Children dress in costume and go house to house begging for candy.

December: Christmas is celebrated on December 25. A people with a deep religious tradition, the Irish concentrate on the religious meaning of the holiday. December 26 is **St. Stephen's Day**, held to honor St. Stephen, the first Christian martyr. The ancient custom of Wren Boys is reenacted. Groups of children, traditional musicians, and Irish dancers perform at neighborhood homes and ask for donations in return for a year of good fortune.

Apple Mash

Ingredients
1 pound cooking apples
2 pounds potatoes
1 tablespoon sugar
2 ounces butter

Directions
Peel the potatoes and cook in salted, boiling water until tender. Peel, core, and thinly slice the apples. Place in a medium saucepan with 1 tablespoon of water and the sugar. Cook until soft.

When potatoes are done, drain well and mash thoroughly. Mix in the cooked apples and the butter. Serve hot.

Shepherd's Pie

The traditional Shepherd's Pie is made with mutton. This version uses ground beef.

Serves 4

Ingredients
2 cups cooked ground beef, well drained
1 tablespoon finely chopped onion
3/4 cup frozen green peas
2 cups beef gravy
salt and pepper
2 cups mashed potatoes, prepared with milk
salt and pepper
1/8 teaspoon of sweet paprika
1 tablespoon butter

Directions
Preheat oven to 400°.

Mix together the ground beef, onion, frozen peas, and gravy. Season with salt and pepper as desired. Pour into a lightly buttered baking dish. Cover with mashed potatoes. Dot the top of the mashed potatoes with butter and sprinkle lightly with paprika. Bake for 30 minutes, or until the potatoes are browned and the pie heated. Let sit for five minutes before serving.

Variation: Mix the paprika with 2 tablespoons of Parmesan cheese before sprinkling on the mashed potatoes.

Irish Potato Candy

Makes 60 pieces

Ingredients
1/4 cup butter, softened
8 ounces cream cheese
1 teaspoon vanilla extract
4 cups confectioners' sugar
2 1/2 cups flaked coconut
1 tablespoon ground cinnamon

Directions
Cream the butter and cream cheese together in a small bowl until very smooth. Add the vanilla. Add the confectioners' sugar 1 cup at a time, beating well after each cup until the mixture is smooth. Using your hands or a wooden spoon, mix in the coconut. Roll into potato shapes and roll in the cinnamon. (If you want a darker color, roll in cinnamon twice.) Place on a waxed-paper-covered baking sheet and chill until set.

Champ

Serves 4

Ingredients
8 medium potatoes, peeled
1 small bunch of scallions
1/2 cup milk
salt and pepper
a generous pat of butter per person

Directions
Boil the potatoes until tender. Drain well, then return to hot pan to dry. Mash well. Keep the potatoes warm while proceeding with the rest of the recipe.

Chop the scallions—green and white parts—finely, and cook in the milk for five minutes. Add the mixture to the mashed potatoes, and beat with a mixer on low until smooth and fluffy. Salt and pepper to taste.

Place a generous portion on each plate. Top with the pat of better. Each forkful of the potatoes should be dipped into the melting butter before eating.

Curach

This is a traditional Irish dessert.

Makes 6 servings.

Ingredients
1 1/2 cups oatmeal
1 cup chopped rhubarb
2 cups raspberries
3 tablespoons honey, divided
2 cups heavy whipping cream

Directions
Preheat the oven to 400°F.

Spread the oatmeal on a nonstick cookie sheet and bake until golden brown, making sure to stir frequently. Set aside to cool.

In a medium saucepan, combine the rhubarb, 1 cup of the raspberries, and 2 tablespoons of the honey. Cook uncovered over medium heat until the rhubarb is tender. Set aside to cool.

In a chilled large mixing bowl, whip the cream until it reaches the stiff peak stage. Gently fold in the remaining honey. Place some of the cream mixture in a trifle bowl or individual glasses. Add a layer of toasted oatmeal, then a layer of the rhubarb mixture, then some fresh raspberries. Repeat. Garnish with more fresh raspberries. Serve chilled.

Project and Report Ideas

Maps

- Make a map of the Republic of Ireland and indicate the country's counties and major cities.
- Make a topographical map of the Republic of Ireland.

Reports

- Research and write a report on Ireland's presidency of the EU.
- Research and write a report on the potato famine.
- Research and write a report on Irish literature and music.
- Research and write a report about the charitable projects of Bono and Bob Geldof.

Biographies
Write a one-page biography of one of the following:

- James Joyce
- Samuel Beckett
- Oscar Wilde
- Bob Geldof

Journal

- Imagine you are living in rural Ireland during the potato famine. Write a journal entry about what life is like for you and your family.
- Imagine you are living in southern Ireland during the Irish Revolution. Write a journal entry describing your everyday life.
- Imagine you have come to the United States to escape the potato famine. Write a journal entry about how your life is different in the new country.
- Imagine that you have seen a leprechaun. Write a journal entry describing your experience.

Projects

- Learn the Gaelic expressions for simple phrases such as hello, good-bye, please, and thank you.
- Go online or to a library and find a picture of an Irish village today. Create a model of one.
- Find an Irish recipe other than the ones in this book and ask an adult to help you make it. Share it with the class.
- Find examples of Irish music and play them for the class.

CHRONOLOGY

7000–6000 BCE	Ireland's first inhabitants arrive.
4000 BCE	Farming is introduced.
500–300 BCE	Celts from eastern Europe arrive in Ireland.
Third and fifth centuries CE	Christianity comes to Ireland.
432 CE	The future saint Patrick arrives in Ireland.
500–800	The Church flourishes in Ireland.
1155	Pope Adrian IV gives King Henry II of England permission to invade Ireland in order to expand the influence of the Roman Church.
1610–1613	Large numbers of English and Scots move onto land taken from the native Irish.
1641	Old English Catholics rebel.
1642	The Anglo-Irish and the native Irish form an alliance called the Confederation of Kilkenny.
1695	Catholics are forbidden to buy land, raise their children as Catholics, carry firearms, or enter the military forces or law.
1697	All bishops and priests are ordered to leave Ireland.
1704	Catholic clergy remaining in Ireland are required to register and swear an oath of allegiance to the English king; a law is passed requiring all members of the Irish Parliament and officeholders to be members of the Church of Ireland.
1727	Catholics lose the right to vote.
1778	The restrictions on Catholics are repealed.
1823	Daniel O'Connell forms the Catholic Association to force the removal of the remaining restrictions on Catholics.
1845	A potato blight hits the country; it lasts for five years.
1870	Isaac Butt founds the Irish Home Government Association.
1886	The first Irish Home Rule bill is introduced in Parliament.
1893	The Gaelic League is formed.
1920	The British Parliament passes the Government of Ireland Act.
1922	Civil war breaks out; it ends in May 1923.
1937	A new constitution is written.
1948	The southern part of the island of Ireland receives its independence from Britain.
1949	The Industrial Development Authority (IDA) is established to promote industrialization.
1973	Ireland joins the European Economic Community (EEC), the forerunner of the European Union (EU).
1990	Mary Robinson is the first woman to be elected president of Ireland.
April 10, 1998	The Good Friday Agreement is signed.
1997	The first legal Irish divorce is obtained.
2002	Ireland becomes the last EU member state to approve expansion plans, which extends membership offers to Eastern European countries.
January 2004	Ireland begins its six-month turn at the presidency of the EU.

FURTHER READING/INTERNET RESOURCES

Cronin, Mike. *History of Ireland*. New York: St. Martin's Press, 2000.

Daly, Ita. *Irish Myths and Legends*. Oxford, U.K.: Oxford University Press, 2001.

Foster, Brett. *James Joyce*. Langhorne, Pa.: Chelsea House, 2003.

Friedman, Lita. *Mary Robinson: Fighter for Human Rights*. Greensboro, N.C.: Avisson Press, 2004.

Moloney, Mick. *Far from the Shamrock Shore: The Story of Irish-American Immigration Through Song*. New York: Crown, 2002.

Travel Information
www.lonelyplanet.com/destinations/europe/ireland
www.travel-guide.com/data/irl/irl.asp

History and Geography
www.irelandstory.com
www.irelandseye.com/aarticles/history/events/index.shtm

Culture and Festivals
www.irelandseye.com
www.emmedici.com/journeys/eire/cultura/ecultura.htm

Economic and Political Information
www.theodora.com/wfbcurrent/ireland
www.freedomhouse.org/research/freeworld/2004/countryratings/ireland.htm

EU Information
europa.eu.int/

FOR MORE INFORMATION

Embassy of Ireland
2234 Massachusetts Avenue NW
Washington, DC 20008
Tel.: 202-462-3939
Fax: 202-232-5993

Embassy of Ireland
Suite 1105, 130 Albert Street
Ottawa K1P 5G4 Ontario
Tel.: 613-233-6281
Fax: 613-233-5835
e-mail: embassyofireland@rogers.com

Embassy of the United States of America
42 Elgin Road
Ballsbridge, Dublin 4, Ireland
Tel.: 353-1-668-8777
Fax: 353-1-668-9946

Consulate of Ireland
345 Park Avenue
New York, NY 10154
Tel.: 212-319-2555
Fax: 212-980-9475

GLOSSARY

Anglo-Normans: Referring to the Normans living in England after 1066.

aristocrats: Members of a country's highest social class.

ascended: Assumed a position of power.

autonomous: Self-governing.

blocs: Groups of countries with shared aims.

cairns: Piles of stones used as markers.

capital: Wealth in the form of money or property.

Celts: Members of an ancient Indo-European people who lived in central and western Europe in pre-Roman times.

clan: A group of families related through a common ancestor or marriage.

creel: A basket designed to hold fish.

dioceses: Districts under the authority of bishops.

drumlins: Long, narrow ridges of gravel and rock left by a moving glacier; one end is blunt and the other tapers.

emancipation: The process or act of freeing someone.

excise: A government-imposed tax on domestic goods.

Gaelic: Relating to any of the Celtic languages of Ireland, Scotland, or the Isle of Man.

gradient: slope.

gross domestic product (GDP): The total value of all goods and services produced in a country in a year, minus net income from investments in other countries.

guerrilla: A member of an irregular paramilitary unit, usually with some political objective.

hydroelectric: Generated by converting the pressure of falling or running water to electricity by means of an engine coupled to a turbine.

illuminated manuscripts: A manuscript in which colorful decorations or illustrations are added to the text.

industrialization: The adoption of industrial means of production and manufacturing.

lichen: Gray, green, or yellow plants appearing on rocks and other surfaces that is a complex organism consisting of fungi and algae growing together in symbiosis.

marauders: Those who wander around carrying out violent attacks in order to steal.

metropolitan: Characteristic of a large city.

monotheism: Belief in one god.

multidenominational: Made up of different religious groups.

papacy: A pope's period of office.

protectionist: A system of duties on imports into a country in order to protect domestic industries.

ratified: Officially approved.

republic: A form of government in which people elect representatives to exercise power for them.

service sectors: Businesses that sell services rather than goods.

solidarity: The act of standing together, presenting a united front.

sovereignty: The right to self-government free from outside interference.

stagnancy: A period of inactivity.

stout: A dark, strong beer.

tariff: Tax levied by governments, usually on imports.

temperate: Not extreme; not too hot and not too cold.

vehemently: With extreme conviction.

vocational: Relating to job or career skills.

INDEX

PICTURE CREDITS

Biographies

Author

Ida Walker is a graduate of the University of Northern Iowa in Cedar Falls. She did graduate work at Syracuse University in New York. Currently, she lives and works in Upstate New York. She is interested in history and learning about new places.

Series Consultants

Ambassador John Bruton served as Irish Prime Minister from 1994 until 1997. As prime minister, he helped turn Ireland's economy into one of the fastest-growing in the world. He was also involved in the Northern Ireland Peace Process, which led to the 1998 Good Friday Agreement. During his tenure as Ireland's prime minister, he also presided over the European Union presidency in 1996 and helped finalize the Stability and Growth Pact, which governs management of the euro. Before being named the European Commission Head of Delegation in the United States, he was a member of the convention that drafted the European Constitution, signed October 29, 2004.

The European Commission Delegation to the United States represents the interests of the European Union as a whole, much as ambassadors represent their countries' interests to the U.S. government. Matters coming under European Commission authority are negotiated between the commission and the U.S. administration.